Original title:
The Winter Solace

Copyright © 2024 Swan Charm
All rights reserved.

Author: Liisi Lendorav
ISBN HARDBACK: 978-9908-1-1816-1
ISBN PAPERBACK: 978-9908-1-1817-8
ISBN EBOOK: 978-9908-1-1818-5

Tapestry Woven in Silver Glow

Under the stars, we gather near,
Laughter dances, bringing cheer.
Threads of joy in colors bright,
Woven tales of festive night.

Crimson ribbons wrap the trees,
Whispers carried on the breeze.
Every face aglow, delight,
Together we embrace the night.

Candles Against the Chill

Flickering flames in windows shine,
Warmth spreads out like sweet old wine.
Softly they chant a timeless song,
Calling loved ones where they belong.

Golden shadows dance on walls,
Nights of joy that time recalls.
Hearts aglow with dreams so bold,
Candles flicker with tales retold.

Silent Whispers of Frost

Frosty breath hangs in the air,
Silent whispers, sweet and rare.
Snowflakes drift with gentle grace,
Painting smiles on every face.

Footprints crunch on paths well-trod,
In the stillness, we feel awed.
Gifts of joy in every flake,
Nature's beauty, make no mistake.

Shadows of the Longest Night

Gather 'round, the fire's glow,
Stories shared, the spirits grow.
Moonlight dances, casting grace,
In this magic, we find our place.

Voices rise in hopeful cheer,
Bringing warmth to those held dear.
Shadows blend and softly sway,
In the night, we find our way.

Night Whispers Beneath the Snow

Under the glow of a silver moon,
Snowflakes dance in a frosty tune.
Laughter mingles with the night air,
Joyful spirits, festive and rare.

Warmth of friendship fills the streets,
Children's laughter, a melody sweet.
Carols echo through the crisp air,
Hearts aglow, love everywhere.

Lanterns Amidst the Season's Quiet

Lanterns flicker with gentle light,
Guiding warmth in the hush of night.
Beneath the stars, we gather near,
Tales of joy that bring us cheer.

Snow blankets the world in white,
Whispers of wonder in pure delight.
Promises made on this starry eve,
Together, we dream and believe.

Frosted Dreams on Winter's Edge

Frosted windows, a canvas bright,
Crafting dreams in the soft twilight.
The crackling fire warms the soul,
Embers dance, making us whole.

Delicate snowflakes in the air,
Each one unique, a beauty fair.
Gathered close, we share a toast,
To laughter and love, we celebrate most.

Light in the Heart of Frost

In the heart of winter's embrace,
Light shines bright, a glowing grace.
Echoing laughter fills the air,
Moments cherished, memories rare.

Bundled tight, we stroll the lane,
Glistening streets where dreams remain.
Hope ignites as we hold on tight,
To the wonders of this festive night.

The Warmth of Solitary Flames

In a circle of light, the embers flicker,
Joyful hearts gather, laughter grows quicker.
Voices mingle, sweet songs take flight,
Under the stars, our spirits ignite.

Marshmallows roast on sticks held high,
As shadows stretch against the night sky.
A symphony shared in warm glow's embrace,
Together we find our rightful place.

Veils of Snowfall and Quietude

Softly the snow descends, pure and bright,
Blanketing earth in a luminous white.
Children's laughter fills the cool air,
Building snowmen with love and care.

Footprints create a tale in the snow,
Dancing around like a gentle flow.
Under the streetlights, glow softly spread,
A cozy warmth spreads, dreams in our heads.

Fables of Ice and Whispered Hues

Icicles dangle, catching the light,
Tales of enchantment dance in the night.
Colors of twilight blend and collide,
As visions of wonder, our hearts abide.

Fables are told, in shadows they play,
Under the moonlight, brightening the way.
Glistening landscapes, a winter's delight,
A canvas of magic, pure and white.

Shadows Dance on Snow-Covered Ground

Whispers of joy in the air take flight,
With every step, our spirits feel light.
The world transformed, a soft lullaby,
In the hush of winter, dreams float high.

Twinkling stars above, so vast and near,
Gentle reminders of warmth and cheer.
Every shadow, a story unfolds,
In the glow of the moon, our hearts become bold.

Paths of Snowflakes and Solitary Thoughts

Gentle flakes drift down, so light,
They dance like whispers in the night.
Blanketing the world in white,
A serene moment, pure delight.

In solitude, I wander free,
With each step, I find the key.
A hush surrounds, just you and me,
In paths where snowflakes come to be.

The stars above begin to gleam,
As shadows fade, I start to dream.
With every breath, I feel the theme,
Of quiet thoughts and soft moonbeam.

This winter's night, so calm, so bright,
The world transformed, a stunning sight.
In paths of snow, I feel the light,
Festive joy in every white.

Twilight's Faithful Companion

As twilight dims, the sky turns fair,
The hues of rose and gold declare.
A companion close, the chill we share,
In laughter light, we find our flare.

The stars begin their nightly show,
With sparkles bright, in ebb and flow.
We stroll through stillness, soft and slow,
In whispers cast, our secrets grow.

In every breeze, a promise swirls,
Through frosty air, the laughter twirls.
We trace the path where joy unfurls,
In twilight's grasp, the heart unfurls.

This festive dusk, serene and sweet,
Where every moment feels complete.
With you beside me, life's a treat,
In twilight's glow, our souls entreat.

Voices Carried by the Winter Wind

The winter wind begins to sing,
With fragile notes that softly cling.
In frosty air, our laughter rings,
A festive joy in everything.

It carries tales from far and wide,
Of snowy hills and riverside.
A chorus bright, our hearts abide,
In winter's arms, we take the ride.

The whispers dance as night draws near,
In every sound, the warmth appears.
We gather close, with smiles sincere,
In harmony, we cast off fear.

These voices shared, they intertwine,
In moments sweet, like vintage wine.
Together here, our spirits shine,
By winter's grace, the world's divine.

The Depths of a Frosty Reverie

In frosty depths, where dreams alight,
The world transforms in pure delight.
A canvas vast, where stars ignite,
In whispers soft, the heart takes flight.

Through silver trees, the shadows play,
As snowflakes weave a glistening way.
In reverie's grip, we laugh and sway,
In magic's hold, the night won't stray.

Each breath we take, a cloud of mist,
A moment seized, a lover's tryst.
In dreams of snow, we can't resist,
A festive tune in frosty bliss.

These depths we share, so warm, so bright,
In winter's grasp, our hearts unite.
With every glance, we feel the light,
In reverie's hold, all feels so right.

The Subtle Art of Letting Go

Bright balloons dance in the air,
Children laugh everywhere.
Colors swirl in joyful cheer,
Embracing moments, drawing near.

A gentle breeze whispers a tune,
As the sun sets, it's almost noon.
With every sigh, a sweet release,
In the heart, we find our peace.

Letting go becomes a game,
Memories flicker, never the same.
In the laughter, the spirit flows,
Finding joy in what we chose.

Radiant Moments in Glistening Cold

Snowflakes twirl in the silver light,
Frosty kisses feel just right.
Laughter echoes, a joyful sound,
In this wonderland, magic is found.

Children bundled, cheeks aglow,
Sleds racing down, spirits in tow.
Each radiant moment sparkles bright,
In glistening cold, pure delight.

Winter's canvas, pure and white,
Every grain a fairy's flight.
With warm hearts, we sing along,
In the glimmer, we belong.

Upon the Frozen Canvas

A canvas vast beneath the sky,
Snowflakes swirl, they softly sigh.
Footprints marked and bright as day,
Ghosts of laughter pave the way.

Gather round, the fire's glow,
Stories shared, warm and slow.
Magical sparkles fill the night,
Hearts aglow with sheer delight.

Each snowman stands with a smile,
A festive spirit spans each mile.
Painting joy on icy seas,
In the moment, time agrees.

Solstice Cannons: A Morning Reverie

The dawn breaks with a colorful boom,
Solstice cannons dispel the gloom.
Golden rays tumble and play,
Welcoming warmth to light our way.

Gathered friends with cups in hand,
Celebrating life, oh isn't it grand?
In every cheer, a hopeful song,
In this moment, we all belong.

Fires crackle, the joy ignites,
Casting spells on winter nights.
Together, hearts entwined and free,
In this reverie, we find our glee.

Stillness of the Winter's Breath

The night is calm, the sky so bright,
Sparkling stars in quiet flight.
Winter's breath, a gentle sway,
Whispers joy on this festive day.

Frosted air with laughter glows,
While twinkling lights bring warmth, it shows.
Families gather, hearts are warm,
Together we brave the winter's charm.

In soft blankets of purest white,
Children play 'neath the moonlight.
Every joy, a shared embrace,
In this stillness, we find our place.

So let us raise our voices high,
In celebration, spirits fly.
For in this winter's breath we find,
A festive peace that warms the mind.

Beneath the Surface of Shimmering Snow

Beneath the surface, magic grows,
In snowflakes dancing, the warmth bestows.
Children laughing, snowballs fly,
Echoes of joy beneath the sky.

Lights are strung from tree to tree,
A sight that fills our hearts with glee.
Generosity like the falling snow,
Covers the world in a golden glow.

Songs of cheer fill the night air,
Voices mingling without a care.
Hot cocoa warms our frozen hands,
While love and laughter fill the lands.

Underneath the bright moon's gaze,
Each moment shines, a sweet praise.
For beneath the surface, we all know,
The magic lies in giving flow.

Echoes of the Long Night

In the hush of the long, cold night,
Echoes dance, hearts take flight.
Songs of old fill the cool air,
Reminders of moments we all share.

Candles flicker, casting shadows wide,
Holding secrets our hearts abide.
Joyful voices rise, a chorus clear,
In this festive gathering, we hold dear.

The fire sparkles, warmth surrounds,
Laughter echoes, love abounds.
For in this night so rich and bright,
We find the magic, pure delight.

The stars align, a festive glow,
Turning the long night into a show.
With every heartbeat, stories told,
In echoes of joy, our spirits unfold.

Starlight Kisses the Snow

Starlight kisses the snowy ground,
A glittering blanket wraps around.
Happy faces, glowing with cheer,
Creating memories we hold dear.

The night ignites with festive cheer,
As laughter sparkles, warm and clear.
Around the fire, stories entwine,
In this moment, our hearts align.

Softly falling, like whispered dreams,
Each flake glistens, or so it seems.
With every laugh, the world aglow,
Magic happens in falling snow.

In unity, our spirits soar,
As starlight whispers forevermore.
This festive night, we come together,
Creating warmth against the weather.

Dreams Wrapped in Icicles

Icicles shimmer, a glistening view,
Children giggle, in skies so blue.
Snowflakes dance on the chilly breeze,
Joyful laughter wraps around trees.

Fireplaces crackle, warmth fills the night,
Memories linger, hearts feel so light.
Gifts all around, each surprise delight,
Shining moments make spirits take flight.

A Pause in Time's Icy Grasp

In winter's embrace, the world holds its breath,
Each twinkling light speaks of magic and zest.
Candles are glowing, their warmth we pursue,
A pause in the moment, all worries subdued.

Snowflakes descend like soft whispers of cheer,
Echoing laughter that fills the whole year.
Families gather, their hearts intertwined,
In a slice of time, pure joy is defined.

Sledding Through the Stillness

Sleds rush downhill, laughter in flight,
Spinning and twirling, pure joy feels so right.
Chilly cheeks rosy, excitement held tight,
Through soft powdery drifts, we soar in delight.

Evening sky glows, a canvas of stars,
Promising dreams wrapped in sweet memoirs.
Hot cocoa awaits, with marshmallows high,
Nights like these make the heart want to fly.

Crystalline Moments of Reflection

Crystal-clear frost paints the world anew,
Every surface gleams with a magical hue.
Laughter and stories spun by the fire,
In crystalline moments, we all feel inspired.

Time holds its breath as we cherish the glow,
Hearts intertwined in a soft, warming flow.
This festive embrace, wrapped in cozy delight,
Promising warmth through this cold winter night.

Beneath the Blanket of White

Snowflakes dance in the air,
Children's laughter fills the night.
Candles glow, twinkling bright,
Beneath the blanket of white.

Joyful hearts gather near,
Sipping cocoa, feeling warm.
Stories shared, spreading cheer,
In this festive winter charm.

Footsteps crunch on the ground,
As carols echo all around.
Hope and love in each sound,
Memories lovingly found.

Under stars, wishes soar,
Together we celebrate fate.
In this moment, we adore,
Beneath the snow, hearts elate.

Solitude's Gentle Embrace

In quiet corners we retreat,
Softly wrapped in silence here.
The world outside, bittersweet,
Yet inside, joy draws near.

Warm blankets on cold nights,
A book, a cup, and dreams align.
Whispers shared with soft delights,
Solitude, a friend of mine.

Candles flicker, shadows play,
As time itself begins to pause.
In this haven, come what may,
Festive spirit finds its cause.

Laughter echoes down the hall,
Memories spun like golden threads.
In our hearts, we're never small,
Solitude, where joy spreads.

Echoes of Quietude

Beneath the stars, we gather 'round,
Whispers soft as the night draws on.
In this space, love is profound,
Echoes of quietude adorn.

The crackling fire warms our souls,
Each ember tells a story bright.
As laughter mingles, joy unfolds,
In the tender glow of light.

Snowflakes drift in gentle clocks,
The world outside still and vast.
In our hearts, time gently knocks,
Forever held, a festive cast.

With every heartbeat, we embrace,
The beauty in the calm and peace.
In the quiet, we find our place,
A celebration that won't cease.

Frosted Dreams and Hushed Hearts

Frosted dreams weave through the night,
Soft whispers of winter's play.
In the moon's soft, silvery light,
Hushed hearts greet the dawning day.

Warming fires and glowing sights,
Gatherings draped in festive cheer.
With each toast, the spirit ignites,
Creating bonds that draw us near.

Snowflakes shimmer, softly bright,
As we dance in the evening's grace.
In this moment, pure delight,
Festive joy we can embrace.

From frosted dreams, we rise and sing,
Celebrating love's gentle art.
In every laugh and every fling,
Our festive souls, never apart.

A Lantern's Glow in Winter's Grasp

Beneath the frost, a light does sway,
A lantern's glow, at close of day.
Snowflakes twirl in joyous dance,
While shadows flicker, hearts enhance.

Children laugh, the warmth ignites,
With every cheer, the world delights.
In cozy nooks, we share our cheer,
As winter's chill draws all near.

The Heartbeat of a Frozen Peace

Silent nights, the world at rest,
A heartbeat hushed, the air is blessed.
Stars like diamonds, bright and clear,
Guide us through a time most dear.

Mittens clasped, we stroll and glide,
In unison, our hearts abide.
With whispers soft, and smiles we trade,
In frosty air, our joys cascade.

Dreams Wrapped in Icy Embrace

Winter whispers through the trees,
Dreams wrapped tight in chilly breeze.
Snow-blanketed paths, we joyfully roam,
Finding warmth in our shared home.

Hot cocoa steams, the fireside gleams,
While laughter twirls through playful dreams.
Each frosty breath, a tale unfold,
In icy nights, our hearts are bold.

Serenity's Chill

In quiet hours, the world slows down,
A serene peace, like a gentle crown.
With every flake that drifts and falls,
We celebrate as winter calls.

Gathered close, our spirits bright,
In the chill, we find our light.
Songs of joy, we softly hum,
In the wonder of winter's drum.

Nurtured in the Chilly Embrace

In the glow of festive lights,
Warm hearts dance in frosty air,
Laughter rings through joyful nights,
As love flows like a gentle prayer.

Children play in snowy lands,
Creating dreams in shimmering white,
With families joining hand in hand,
Together, they embrace the night.

Cocoa brews with marshmallows sweet,
Gifts wrapped tight with ribbons bright,
While carols sway to the cheerful beat,
The chilly embrace feels just right.

As stars twinkle and snowflakes swirl,
Hope ignites the wintry scene,
In this moment, hearts unfurl,
A festive warmth in the serene.

Rebirth in the Icy Cradle

Amidst the frost, the world awakes,
A canvas blank, with snowflakes spun,
In the chill, a new path makes,
Celebration has just begun.

Glistening trees dressed up so fine,
Glow with colors, bright and bold,
Underneath the sparkling pine,
Stories of joy and love unfold.

Families gather, the warmth they share,
Moments cherished, around the fire,
With every laugh, the spark fills air,
Hearts ignited, lifting higher.

As the icy cradle holds the night,
Hope blooms bright in the chilly glow,
Every spirit takes joyful flight,
In the embrace of winter's show.

Where Silence Fills the Air

In the stillness, whispers play,
Snowflakes waltz, a silent choir,
Every moment holds the sway,
Of hope and love, lifting higher.

Candles flicker, casting spells,
In the hush, each smile grows wide,
Stories wrapped in gentle bells,
In this peace, our souls abide.

With every shadow softly deep,
The night embraces festive cheer,
Dreams awoken from their sleep,
Where silence sings for all to hear.

As the moon glows, a guiding light,
Hearts entwined in the winter's air,
In the silence, pure delight,
A joyful hymn, beyond compare.

Chasing Shadows in the Frosty Twilight

As twilight falls, the shadows play,
Dancing light on snowy ground,
In the chill, we laugh and sway,
Festival joy is all around.

Footprints mark our secret trails,
In the frost, we chase our dreams,
Laughter echoes, never pales,
As starlit nights weave golden seams.

Each moment precious, time stands still,
Underneath the vast, bright sky,
Hearts ignited, we seek the thrill,
Chasing shadows, as spirits fly.

In frosty twilight, joy aligns,
With every glance, the warmth we share,
Together, under these starlit signs,
In our hearts, we feel the fair.

Tranquility's Veil of White

A blanket of snow wraps the earth,
Soft whispers echo, celebrating mirth.
Lights twinkle brightly, a festive show,
As laughter and joy like sweet rivers flow.

The trees wear crowns of shimmering white,
Their branches dancing in pure delight.
Children build snowmen, warm and round,
In this magical world, joy can be found.

Footprints are left in the sparkling dew,
Each mark a story, a wish coming true.
Hot cocoa steams in the winter air,
Creating memories that we all share.

As dusk settles softly, the stars ignite,
Festive spirits soar, shimmering bright.
Under the glow of the moonlit night,
We're wrapped in tranquility, pure and light.

Frost-Kissed Moments

When morning breaks with a frosty hue,
The world awakens with wonders anew.
Ice crystals dance on the window's frame,
Each moment treasured, never the same.

Frosty breaths puff like clouds in the cold,
Stories of warmth through the ages told.
Families gather, bonds strong and tight,
In the heart of winter, everything feels right.

Laughter mingles with the crackle of fire,
In the cozy embrace, our spirits aspire.
Gifts wrapped in ribbons of red and gold,
Frost-kissed moments, together we hold.

The evening glows with a magical air,
Soft carols sung, while hearts lay bare.
Under the stars where the laughter keeps,
In the warmth of love, tranquility sleeps.

Serenity of the Frozen Dusk

As day bids farewell to the softly blue,
The sky paints a canvas, a charming view.
Gentle snowflakes drift, dance in the breeze,
Wrapping the world in serenity's freeze.

The twilight whispers secrets untold,
While sparkles of starlight in silence unfold.
The night drapes a shawl of hope and cheer,
In frozen dusk, our spirits draw near.

Families gather, hearts full of grace,
Hot cider in hand, a warm embrace.
Stories around the crackling fire,
Each shared laugh ignites our desire.

With every twinkle of joy in the dark,
We chase the chill with love's gentle spark.
As the world slows down, dreams take flight,
In the serenity of the frozen night.

A Treetop Symphony of Snow

Up high in the treetops, a symphony plays,
Snowflakes like notes in a frosty ballet.
Branches sway gently, the wind sings along,
Nature's own chorus, pure, sweet, and strong.

The night holds a hush, magic in the air,
Each breath an echo of love and care.
Families embrace under starlit skies,
In the warmth of each heart, the true joy lies.

Sparkling lights twinkle on every embrace,
In every soft flake, we find our place.
Treetops adorned in their white, pure best,
With a symphony of snow, all troubles rest.

The music of winter, a tranquil score,
In each lovely note, we always want more.
As laughter rings out, beneath the moon's glow,
We dance with delight in this treetop show.

Stillness Breathing Under Ice

The world is wrapped in icy dreams,
A hush that blankets all that gleams.
Beneath the frost, life's whispers sigh,
As time dances slow, beneath the sky.

Snow-laden branches lightly sway,
In winter's grasp, they find their play.
The shimmering light, a jeweled embrace,
In this stillness, warmth finds its place.

Sparkling moments weaved in frost,
Amidst the silence, love is embossed.
Laughter echoes, a soft refrain,
In stillness breathing, joy remains.

With every breath, a story spun,
Frozen crystals glow in the sun.
Together we bask in this embrace,
In stillness breathing, finding grace.

Snowflakes Dance in Silence

Snowflakes twirl in a silent flight,
Whispering secrets, pure and bright.
In gentle spirals, they play and prance,
Nature's own rhythm, a winter dance.

The world adorned in white so thick,
Each flake a dream, with magic to pick.
Soft laughter joins the sparkling hue,
In this festive moment, hearts feel new.

Children gather, their faces aglow,
Catching the flakes, letting joy flow.
In the silence, a harmony reigns,
Snowflakes dance, washing away pains.

A blanket of quiet, a world at peace,
In every flake, a sweet release.
As snowflakes fall, the spirit's free,
Together we cherish, in jubilee.

The Calm Before the Stargazing

Twilight whispers, the day takes a bow,
Stars peek shyly, beneath a soft gown.
The world is hushed in a soothing balm,
In this calm, the night feels warm.

Candles flicker with a gentle light,
Casting shadows that dance through the night.
In shared silence, our hearts prepare,
For the starlit wonders that soon will flare.

Gathered together, we share our dreams,
Under the cosmos where magic gleams.
In this stillness, connections weave,
As we gaze upwards, hearts believe.

The calm before all beauty unfolds,
A tapestry of dreams and stories told.
In this precious moment, let us stay,
Together in wonder, come what may.

Unraveled Threads of Winter

Threads of winter unravel and play,
In colors of twilight, they dance and sway.
Each stitch a memory, woven with care,
In cozy corners, love fills the air.

Scarves and mittens, warm and bright,
Wrap us in comfort through the night.
Fires crackle, their warmth draws near,
In the heart of winter, we gather cheer.

The laughter of friends, a welcoming sound,
In this festive season, joy knows no bound.
Songs fill the air, like whispers of dreams,
In unraveled threads, unity beams.

With every moment, our hearts intertwine,
In the tapestry of life, a love divine.
Winter may chill, but souls ignite,
In unraveled threads, we find our light.

Echoes of Solitude in White

Snowflakes dance and twirl,
Bringing whispers of the night.
In the hush, a soft pearl,
Alone yet feeling light.

Footprints mark a fleeting trace,
Laughter woven in the air.
Winter's chill, an embrace,
Silence sings without a care.

Trees adorned in glittering frost,
A canvas pure, serene and bright.
For every joy, a dream is lost,
In solitude, we find the light.

Echoes linger, soft and sweet,
As shadows play on frozen ground.
Each heartbeat, a rhythmic beat,
In this white world, peace is found.

Candlelight Against the Snow

Flickering flames in the dark,
Warmth radiates through the night.
Outside sings the winter lark,
While shadows dance in delight.

Glowing embers in each room,
Stories shared, hearts entwined.
Against the cold, we find our bloom,
In candlelight, love is blind.

Cheery laughter fills the space,
Joy ignites with every spark.
Winter's chill, a soft embrace,
Together we leave our mark.

The world wrapped in snowy white,
We gather close, hearts aglow.
In the stillness, pure delight,
Candlelight against the snow.

Charmed by Winter's Sigh

Softly falls the evening light,
Winter breathes a gentle tune.
Stars awake, twinkling bright,
Underneath the silver moon.

Magic lingers in the air,
Snowflakes shimmer, pure and sweet.
The world feels light, free from care,
Charmed by winter, hearts do meet.

Cozy fires crackle near,
Blankets wrap us, snug and warm.
In each glance, love draws near,
A tranquil night, safe from harm.

Holding on to whispered dreams,
In the silence, joy does grow.
Charmed we are, as time redeems,
By winter's sigh, we feel the glow.

Echos of Forgotten Dreams

In the frost, old wishes gleam,
Echoes dance in the crisp air.
Memories flow like a stream,
Whispering tales of those who care.

Shimmering lights in the night,
Hold the hopes that once took flight.
Sparkle bright, a sweet delight,
In a quiet world bathed in white.

Underneath the starry dome,
Secrets shared in softest light.
Laughter calls us back to home,
Feelings grow bold, taking flight.

In this moment, dreams resound,
A symphony of joy and cheer.
In winter's arms, we're tightly bound,
Echoes of dreams, forever near.

Echoes of the Frozen Hearth

Laughter rings through the frosty air,
Warm fires crackle, casting a glow.
Families gather, hearts laid bare,
Sharing tales from long ago.

The table is adorned with delight,
Plates piled high, joy fills the room.
Candles flicker in the soft twilight,
Ever banishing the winter's gloom.

Outside, the world is draped in white,
Snowflakes dance in a playful spree.
Joyful spirits take to the night,
As echoes of laughter set them free.

In this frozen landscape, hearts are bright,
With every hug, warmth grows anew.
In the hearth's embrace, love takes flight,
Fires burn bright, and friendships true.

Nightfall in a Crystal World

Stars begin to twinkle above,
The sky draped in velvet hue.
Whispers of magic, like a dove,
Nature's secrets to pursue.

Frosty paths lightly crunch beneath,
Glowing lanterns guide the way.
A hush of wonder, silken wreath,
As night transforms the end of day.

Every branch is cloaked in frost,
Crystals glimmer with a dream.
Unlike any treasure we've lost,
Nightfall reigns with gentle gleam.

Joy spins through the chilly air,
With every step, a dance of fate.
Together we revel without a care,
In this crystal world, we celebrate.

Veil of Shimmering Silence

A blanket of snow, soft and wide,
Covers the earth like a tender embrace.
In this calm, our joys we confide,
As laughter echoes through time and space.

Moonlight spills on frozen streams,
Whispers of wishes brush the night.
Every shadow ignites our dreams,
Wrapped in the glow of silver light.

Beneath the veil of shimmering silence,
Hearts connect in the quiet bliss.
Moments echo, full of reliance,
In this stillness, we find our kiss.

The world holds its breath in delight,
As we cherish what truly binds.
In the depths of this magical night,
Love's gentle warmth is what we find.

Frosted Leaves and Faded Dreams

Frosted leaves fluttering down,
Whisper tales of seasons past.
They twirl lightly, wearing a crown,
Marked by memories that hold fast.

Each breath mingles with the cold,
As warmth ignites from fires near.
In our hearts, stories unfold,
Together we share our festive cheer.

Stockings hung with love and care,
Gifts wrapped tight, smiles abound.
In this circle, joy we share,
With every laugh, our hearts resound.

As twilight deepens, stars ignite,
And dreams take flight on winter's breath.
In this embrace, our spirits light,
Frosted leaves dance in the shadow of death.

Dreams Unfurled in Ice

In the twilight glow, dreams take flight,
Sparkling like stars on a winter night.
Laughter dances on the frosty air,
As joy unravels everywhere.

Snowflakes twirl in a merry ballet,
Whispers of magic in the light of day.
Children's cheer echoes through the pines,
In this frozen land where love intertwines.

The world's a canvas, painted in white,
Each breath a whisper, soft and light.
Together we cherish this festive embrace,
In dreams unfurled, we find our place.

With every heartbeat, the cold feels warm,
In the heart of winter, we gather, we swarm.
Let the shimmering beauty guide our cheer,
As we cradle the warmth of the season near.

Chilling Beauty Beneath the Stars

Beneath the stars, a tranquil scene,
Whispers of winter, pristine and keen.
Glittering snow paints the ground below,
In the night's embrace, our spirits glow.

The moonlight dances on icy streams,
Wrapped in wonder, lost in dreams.
Laughter bubbles like sparkling wine,
In this chilling beauty, hearts align.

Fireflies of frost, in the cold night,
Illuminate paths, weaving delight.
With siblings and friends, under the skies,
We weave our tales, where joy never dies.

As echoes of merriment fill the air,
We celebrate moments, banish despair.
In this frosty realm, we find our bliss,
Embracing the night with warmth and a kiss.

The Wisp of Frosty Twilight

In twilight's cloak, the world breathes slow,
Wistful whispers of winds that blow.
Frosty tendrils curl like lace,
As we gather in this magical place.

The air is filled with laughter's chime,
Echoing sweetly, transcending time.
A tapestry woven with stories bright,
In the embrace of this frosty twilight.

Candles flicker in the gentle breeze,
Casting shadows that dance with ease.
In the midst of winter, our spirits soar,
Finding peace in the laughter we adore.

The misty breath of joy we share,
Draws us closer in the crisp cold air.
Under the stars, with hearts so light,
We weave our dreams in frosty twilight.

Embracing the Icy Solitude

In icy solitude, beauty is found,
The whispering winds gently surround.
Snowflakes descend, a delicate race,
Embracing the stillness, a sacred space.

Stars twinkle brightly in the quiet night,
We revel in solitude, hearts feeling light.
The world slows down, a lullaby sung,
In this frosty haven, we feel so young.

Time drips like icicles, slow but sure,
In this charming pause, our spirits pur.
With every breath, the cold feels bright,
As we cradle warmth in the depth of night.

Together we gather, both near and afar,
In the icy embrace, under the stars.
With cheeks aglow, we dance and sway,
Embracing the joy, come what may.

Twilight's Icy Grip

As twilight falls, the world aglow,
With twinkling lights that dance below.
Laughter weaves through crisp, cool air,
A festive spirit, everywhere.

The frosty ground beneath our feet,
We share our joy, a bond so sweet.
With cups of cheer held up on high,
We toast to dreams that light the sky.

In this embrace, time seems to freeze,
As hearts unite with joyful ease.
Beneath the stars, we spin and twirl,
In winter's grasp, our flags unfurl.

So let the icy grip hold tight,
In every soul shines pure delight.
For in this moment, pure and right,
We forge our paths in buzzing night.

A Breath of Air in Frigid Stillness

With every breath, a cloud appears,
Warming smiles amid the cheers.
In frigid stillness, warmth ignites,
As flickering flames bring cozy nights.

We gather close, our spirits bright,
Adventures shared under the moonlight.
The crispness sparkles in the glow,
Of winter tales we've come to know.

Chilled hands clasped in loving grip,
In this serene, nostalgic trip.
Joy bounces through the frozen air,
As laughter dances everywhere.

So let us savor every chime,
In joyful harmony and rhyme.
For in this season, we will play,
And chase the clouds of winter away.

Frosted Memories in Dusk's Embrace

In dusk's embrace, the world feels still,
Frosted memories a heart can fill.
Each frosted breath a whispered thought,
Of moments cherished, lessons taught.

The lanterns sway with soft cheer's glow,
As tales of yore begin to flow.
With every glance, a story shared,
Of snowy paths we boldly dared.

A dance of shadows, twinkling light,
We gather 'round, hearts feeling bright.
In laughter's warmth, we find our way,
Through frosty nights and playful day.

So let us wrap ourselves in joy,
As winter's chill is but a ploy.
To gather close and celebrate,
The magic that we cultivate.

Harmony in the Gentle Freeze

The gentle freeze wraps every soul,
In this vast world, we feel quite whole.
Winter winds bring melodies clear,
Companions cheer, as spring draws near.

With every step, the frosty crunch,
We clutch our mugs and share our lunch.
In harmony, hearts beat as one,
Under the glow of the warming sun.

Every giggle flutters like snow,
Tracing paths where warm hearts flow.
The festive mood lights up our eyes,
As love and laughter fill the skies.

So let this harmony hold fast,
Embrace the chill; let joy be cast.
For in this season's sweet refrain,
We gather warmth through every strain.

Embracing the Chill

Snowflakes dance on winter's breeze,
Children's laughter, joyous, free.
Warm mugs held close, families cheer,
Together we toast, end of the year.

Glowing lights adorn the streets,
Every corner a memory greets.
Soft whispers in the frosty air,
Magic weaves through moments shared.

Footprints trace a playful path,
In the chill, we find our laugh.
Joyful hearts in winter's embrace,
Celebrating life, our sacred space.

As the night falls, stars will shine,
Fires crackle, spirits intertwine.
Embracing the chill, all feels right,
In this warmth, oh, what a night!

Moonlit Elegy of Ice

Under the moon, the world aglow,
Icy branches, a shimmering show.
A gentle hush blankets the earth,
In this stillness, we find rebirth.

Whispers of night in the frosted air,
Soft croonings stir, free from care.
Laughter weaves 'neath the silver beam,
In dreams of warmth, we dare to dream.

Stars twinkle above in cosmic delight,
Guiding souls through the velvet night.
Nature's beauty, a frozen waltz,
In moonlit elegance, no faults.

Together we stand, hearts entwined,
In the silence, solace we find.
An elegy sung for the sparkling ice,
In this moment, all feels nice.

A Stillness Beneath the Snow

A blanket white where silence reigns,
Each flake whispers, soft refrains.
Amidst the stillness, joy unfurls,
As laughter echoes 'round the world.

Children frolic, their spirits bright,
Building castles in pale moonlight.
With rosy cheeks, they dash and play,
In this winter wonderland, we sway.

Hot cocoa warms our eager hands,
While stories weave in cozy strands.
Beneath the snow, hope does bloom,
In this frosted, joyful room.

As night drapes its velvety cloak,
Around the fire, spirits stoke.
A stillness found in snowy grace,
Together, we find our sacred space.

Embrace of the Frosted Dawn

Morning breaks with a frosted glow,
Sunrise dances on white below.
A chill in the air, yet hearts so warm,
In this dawn, we weather the storm.

Birds chirp sweetly from tree to tree,
Whispers of hope in harmony.
With every breath, we feel alive,
In this embrace, we know we thrive.

Glistening paths invite our stride,
In nature's wonder, we take pride.
Through fields of pearls, we run and play,
In the joy of life, we find our way.

Frosted dawn, a canvas bright,
Capturing dreams as day ignites.
In your embrace, we feel the cheer,
Together in this moment, dear.

Serenity Found in White Stillness

Snowflakes dance in gentle flight,
Blanketing the earth in white.
Children's laughter fills the air,
Joy abounds without a care.

Twinkling lights adorn the trees,
Whispers carried by the breeze.
Hot cocoa warms our chilly hands,
As winter's magic softly stands.

Fires crackle, stories shared,
In this moment, hearts are bared.
Harmony in every sight,
Serenity found in white.

The world in slumber, calm and bright,
Embraced by winter's sweet delight.
In the stillness, peace abounds,
In snowy realms, our joy resounds.

A Tapestry of Snowflakes

Each flake a gem that softly falls,
Creating magic, nature calls.
Colors twinkle like a dream,
A tapestry, it seems.

Here we gather, friends unite,
Wrapped in warmth, hearts feel light.
Smiles and laughter fill the night,
In this wondrous festive sight.

Children play, their voices soar,
Rolling snowballs on the floor.
Chasing shadows in the glow,
Of the moonlit world below.

With every flake that graces ground,
A piece of joy can always be found.
In this winter's grand embrace,
A tapestry of love and grace.

Where Frost Meets Reflection

The world adorned in icy lace,
Mirroring the joy we chase.
Nights filled with laughter and song,
In this festive place, we belong.

Reflections dance upon the stream,
Like tiny stars that brightly gleam.
Footprints trace a story new,
Where the frost and dreams come true.

Crisp air filled with cheerful cheer,
Echoes of love drawing near.
Every moment, shared with care,
In the glow of winter's flare.

Here in warm and fleeting light,
We celebrate this snowy night.
Where frost meets joy and delight,
In our hearts, everything feels right.

In the Arms of the Silent Deep

Underneath the starry sky,
Winter whispers gently by.
Holding warmth in hearts of kin,
As laughter bubbles from within.

In the hush, we hear the sound,
Of joyful spirits all around.
Candles flicker, casting light,
In the arms of the silent night.

Gathered close, our stories blend,
Creating memories, sweet as friend.
Quiet moments, richly steeped,
In the arms of the silent deep.

Sledding down the hills of white,
Filling days with pure delight.
Together, winter dreams we keep,
In the arms of love, we leap.

Moonlit Silence Over Frozen Fields

Beneath the moon's soft, silver glow,
The frozen fields in whispers flow.
Stars twinkle bright in the frosty air,
A night of magic, beyond compare.

The world wears a blanket, pure and white,
As shadows dance in the soft moonlight.
Echoes of laughter lift through the trees,
Carried away on a gentle breeze.

Snowflakes twirl like glittering dreams,
Adorning the night with shimmering beams.
Together we revel in winter's embrace,
Finding our joy in this serene space.

Oh, festive heart, in the still of night,
Breathe in the beauty, heart so light.
Moonlit silence wraps all around,
In frozen fields, our love is found.

Last Light's Lullaby

As daylight fades with a golden hue,
The sky transforms, a canvas anew.
Whispers of dusk in a soft refrain,
A lullaby sung by the evening rain.

Soft shadows stretch, a gentle sigh,
While fireflies blink like stars in the sky.
The world slows down, a tranquil pause,
Embracing the night, we find our cause.

Each moment wrapped in twilight's glow,
As laughter dances, sweet and slow.
We gather 'round, the warmth we share,
Under the stars, love fills the air.

In the hush of night, we feel alive,
In every heart, the joy will thrive.
Last light's lullaby, so sweet and clear,
A festive serenade that draws us near.

Tender Frosts and Silent Stars

The night enfolds in tender frost,
A blanket of peace, where dreams are tossed.
Silent stars twinkle with gentle grace,
Guiding our hearts to this sacred place.

In whispers soft, the night does sing,
As frosty winds weave a magical string.
Each breath a cloud in the chilly night,
A moment captured in pure delight.

Together we wander, hand in hand,
Under the glow of a snowy land.
Joy fills the air like a sweet perfume,
In the tender frost, our spirits bloom.

With laughter echoing through the dark,
We celebrate life, each flickering spark.
Tender frosts and silent stars align,
In this festive moment, your heart meets mine.

Serenity in the Stillness

In the stillness, the world finds peace,
Moments of joy that never cease.
Fresh fallen snow wraps all in white,
A canvas of calm, pure and bright.

Fires crackle softly, warmth surrounds,
Laughter erupts in the quiet sounds.
We raise our glasses to the night ahead,
Celebrating the memories we've thread.

With each glimmer, the stars align,
In this serene glow, our hearts entwine.
A festive spirit fills the air,
With love's sweet whispers, we joyfully share.

Let the stillness embrace our dreams,
As holiday magic flows in streams.
Serenity found in every glance,
In life's great tapestry, we joyously dance.

Portraits of a Winter's Heart

In the glow of festive lights,
Snowflakes dance with pure delight.
Children laugh, their joy rings clear,
In winter's arms, love draws near.

Carols echo through the night,
Fires crackle, spirits bright.
Warmth within, despite the chill,
Heartfelt moments, time stands still.

Each breath steams in frosty air,
Gathered close, we share, we care.
A portrait fine of joy and mirth,
Crafted from this winter's hearth.

With every glow, the magic grows,
In these smiles, the warmth flows.
A tapestry of love we weave,
In winter's heart, we all believe.

Snowbound Reflections

Snowfall whispers soft and low,
Blankets white on world below.
Window panes dressed up in lace,
A festive cheer, a warm embrace.

Candles flicker, shadows play,
In the dark, we find our way.
With cups in hand, we toast to life,
To loved ones near, to joy, no strife.

Reflections dance on crystal bright,
Each moment shines, a pure delight.
In winter's calm, our hearts align,
In every breath, love's sweet design.

Together we share this sacred space,
Embracing warmth in every face.
Upon this canvas white and vast,
We paint our joy, a love that lasts.

In the Heart of the Frosted Realm

In the heart of winter's hold,
Stories whispered, tales retold.
Frosty branches, glistening white,
A canvas painted with purest light.

Music flows from every street,
Joyful faces, strangers meet.
With laughter bright as twinkling stars,
We gather close, forgetting scars.

Snowflakes fall like gentle sighs,
Underneath the wintry skies.
Every moment wrapped in bliss,
A festive charm, not one we'd miss.

In gentle shades of silver grey,
The world transforms, in grand display.
In this realm where magic's found,
A winter's heart, forever bound.

A Glimmer in the Frost

A glimmer shines, a promise bright,
In icy realms, hearts take flight.
Joyful songs fill frosty air,
In every note, we rise, we share.

With every step in piles of snow,
The warmth of laughter starts to flow.
Gathered around the fire's glow,
A tapestry of love to show.

In this freeze, our spirits soar,
Embracing all that we adore.
From every heart, a glimmer seen,
In winter's grasp, we chase the dream.

So let us hold this moment dear,
With every laugh, we draw near.
In frosted realms, our joys entwine,
A festive love, forever shine.

Solstice Reflections in a Lonely Land

In the stillness of the night, light gleams,
Candles flicker, dance in gentle streams.
A chill in the air, laughter so bright,
Hearts come alive in the warmth of the light.

Snowflakes twirl like confetti in flight,
Gathering hope beneath the moonlight.
Voices unite in songs soft and true,
Celebrations rise, a joy to renew.

Footprints in snow lead to cozy halls,
Where memories linger, love gently calls.
The spirit of giving envelops us whole,
Together we share, reaching each soul.

As stars twinkle down, the night is aglow,
Festive spirits awaken, merriment flows.
A toast to the moments, the laughter we know,
In this lonely land, together we grow.

Beneath a Sky of Whispered Stars

Under the blanket of a star-speckled sky,
Whispers of joy float gently by.
Firelight crackles, warmth wraps around,
In this tranquil space, love can be found.

The night is alive with stories untold,
Promises shimmer, like silver and gold.
Each twinkling star sings a lullaby,
Beneath its embrace, we soar and fly.

Laughter and cheer fill the crisp, cool air,
In every shared moment, life's treasures bare.
We gather as one, hearts open and free,
A festive reminder of the joy we see.

As we dance in the glow of the starlit night,
Each step we take feels perfectly right.
Beneath a celestial canvas, we stand,
Together we weave a jubilant band.

The Embrace of Cold Shadows

In the hush of twilight, shadows embrace,
A festive spirit fills this quiet space.
Lights twinkle softly, hearts beat as one,
Under the canvas where joy has begun.

Frosted windows tell tales of delight,
As laughter escapes into the cool night.
With every moment, memories are spun,
The dance of the season has only begun.

Snow blankets all in a shimmering hue,
Unity flourishes, we gather anew.
With mugs full of warmth, we share and we cheer,
The beauty of friendship brings everyone near.

The cold shadows beckon, yet we feel so warm,
Wrapped in the melodies of life's festive charm.
Each embrace a promise, each smile a song,
In the heart of the winter, we all belong.

Serenity in the Snowbound Silence

In a world wrapped tight in soft, white snow,
Silence whispers secrets only we know.
A blanket of calm, it covers the earth,
In this serene stillness, we find rebirth.

With candles aglow, we gather around,
In this peaceful moment, love can be found.
Each laugh shared, a spark in the night,
A testament to warmth in the frosty light.

Snowflakes drift lightly, like whispers in air,
As hearts entwine gently, free from despair.
We celebrate life with joy all around,
In the embrace of this snowbound ground.

Together we weave our dreams into light,
Creating a tapestry, bold and bright.
Serenity reigns in the stillness we find,
In the snowy embrace of this festive kind.

Lullabies in the Frosty Dusk

Softly the snowflakes twirl and dance,
Underneath the fading twilight's glance.
Children's laughter fills the chilly air,
As winter's blanket wraps us with care.

Lanterns flicker, casting golden light,
While shadows play in the gentle night.
Hot cocoa steams in cozy mugs,
A festive glow, with warmth that hugs.

Songs of joy rise with every cheer,
Echoes of love that we hold dear.
As carols blend with the soft night breeze,
Our hearts are lifted, our spirits at ease.

Beneath the stars, we hum along,
In this moment, we all belong.
Together we sing, in harmony true,
Lullabies sweet, for me and for you.

Respite Beneath the Snowy Canopy

Whispers of winter soft as a sigh,
Coated in white, the world glimmers shy.
Treetops adorned in a crystal lace,
Nature's beauty, a serene embrace.

Footprints crunch on the fresh-fallen snow,
Children trailing where laughter will flow.
Snowmen stand guard, with hats all askew,
Creating a scene, pure and brand new.

Sleds glide down hills, in jubilant waves,
Echoing joy in the frosty caves.
With mittens and scarves, we bundle tight,
In the magic of this sparkling night.

Fireside tales make the heart feel whole,
As embers flicker, igniting the soul.
Beneath the canopy of dreams divine,
We cherish these moments, forever shine.

Echoing Stillness of the Frozen Hour

A hush blankets all in a silvery hue,
Where time gently pauses, bright and anew.
Frosted branches creak in the chilly air,
Holding the secrets that winter lays bare.

Moonlight dances on the frozen lake,
Reflecting glimmers, like stars that quake.
In stillness profound, we breathe in deep,
Awash in a magic that lulls us to sleep.

Crystals shimmer in the quiet night,
Nature's canvas, painted with light.
The heart finds peace in the calm of it all,
In the echoing stillness, we rise and fall.

Together we marvel at this frozen hour,
Feeling the warmth of a newfound power.
In whispered tones, our hopes intertwine,
As dreams take flight, in this moment divine.

Secrets Whispered by the Ice

In the still of the night, when the world sleeps tight,
The ice holds secrets, hidden from sight.
Glistening surfaces, a mirror so clear,
Reflecting our wishes, bringing us near.

Under the moon's gaze, stories unfold,
Of winter's enchantment, forever retold.
Skaters glide softly, a ballet so grand,
Painting the cold with each graceful hand.

The nights are alive with a shimmering tune,
As laughter and joy swim beneath the moon.
Fires crackle, summoning warmth from within,
We share the treasures, through thick and thin.

So gather close, let the tales ignite,
Secrets of ice fill the magical night.
In festive whispers, our hearts beat as one,
Through winter's embrace, our journey's begun.

Silent Shadows of Frosted Nights

Beneath the moon's soft glowing light,
Children laugh, hearts feel so bright.
Stars above like diamonds twinkle,
In winter's chill, joy makes us sprinkle.

The air is crisp, the world adorned,
By glistening snow, a scene reborn.
Laughter dances on every breeze,
In frosted nights, our souls find ease.

Colors of warmth in every smile,
Together we celebrate in style.
Hot cocoa warms our eager hands,
As love and laughter fill the lands.

Silent shadows play in the light,
The world aglow, a festive sight.
With every heart, the spirit grows,
In frosted nights, the magic flows.

Embrace of the Longest Night

Underneath the velvet skies,
Candles flicker, love never dies.
Gathered close, we share our dreams,
In the warmth, our laughter beams.

Fires crackle, stories unfold,
In the night, our hearts grow bold.
Tales of old and wishes new,
In the darkest hour, hope shines through.

With every hug, we feel the cheer,
In the embrace of those we hold dear.
The longest night, a cherished cry,
As warmth and bliss drift to the sky.

Stars alight in joyous sight,
In the embrace of this special night.
Together we rise, hand in hand,
In the glow of love, forever we stand.

Whispers in the Snow

Gentle flakes fall, a soft embrace,
In the silence, we find our place.
Footprints linger, stories told,
As winter's magic begins to unfold.

Children's laughter fills the air,
Whispers of joy held everywhere.
Snowmen smiling, a whimsical sight,
In the land of white, hearts feel light.

The world transformed, a canvas bright,
With every glance, pure delight.
Sleds racing down hills so steep,
In wintry dreams, our spirits leap.

Whispers in the snow, secrets shared,
In every flake, love is declared.
With open hearts, we revel and play,
In winter's wonder, we'll find our way.

Chill of the Dimming Sun

As daylight fades, the chill comes near,
Gathering friends, we draw them near.
Glowing fire pits, laughter flows,
In twilight's glow, warmth gently grows.

Shadows dance with the setting sun,
In chilly air, the joy's begun.
Spirits high in the crisp night air,
Wrapped in blankets, without a care.

Hot drinks steaming in our hands,
As the evening magic expands.
Stories shared by the flickering light,
In the chill of dusk, everything feels right.

Embracing moments, memories to hold,
In the dimming sun, our hearts turn gold.
With every laugh, the night unfolds,
In the chill of the dimming, love beholds.

www.ingramcontent.com/pod-product-compliance
Lightning Source LLC
LaVergne TN
LVHW011735140125
801271LV00003B/43